THE ANCIENT WORLD

ROME

Sean Sheehan and Pat Levy

WAYLAND

THE ANCIENT WORLD

THE AZTECS · BENIN AND OTHER AFRICAN KINGDOMS EGYPT · GREECE · THE INCAS · ROME

Produced for Wayland (Publishers) Limited by
Roger Coote Publishing
Gissing's Farm, Fressingfield, Eye
Suffolk IP21 5SH, England

Editor: Alex Edmonds
Series editor: Alex Woolf
Designer: Victoria Webb
Map artwork: Peter Bull

First published in 1998 by
Wayland (Publishers) Limited, 61 Western Road
Hove, East Sussex BN3 1JD, England

Find Wayland on the internet at http://www.wayland.co.uk

Cover pictures: Marble bust portrait of Augustus (left), and Roman wall mosaic from Pompeii showing a ferry boat.

British Library Cataloguing in Publication Data
Sheehan, Sean and Levy, Patricia
    Rome. – (The ancient world)
    1.Rome – Juvenile literature
    I.Title
    937.6

ISBN 0 7502 2084 8

Printed and bound in Italy by
G. Canale & C.S.p.A., Turin

Picture acknowledgements: Ronald Sheridan Ancient Art and Architecture Collection Ltd. 1, 8, 9, 16, 17, 20–21, 25, 26, 32, 33, 34, 39, 42–43, 46, 48, 59 (middle); C.M.Dixon front cover (right), 5, 10, 12 (top), 12 (bottom), 15, 18, 22, 24–25 (middle), 27, 28–29, 30, 37 (top), 41, 44, 47, 51, 52, 54, 59 (top); E.T. Archive front cover (left), 6, 7 (Archaeological Museum Naples), 35 (Prestino Museum, Rome), 36 49 (National Glyptothek Munich), 53 (bottom right), 56 (San Vitale Ravenna Italy); Werner Forman Archive 31, 45, 50 (J.Paul Getty Museum, Malibu), 55, 60.

Contents

CHAPTER 1

Early Rome

In only 1,000 years, ancient Rome created the greatest Empire that the world had ever seen. It was not only the size of the empire that was so impressive, but also its ability to take on all the best aspects of the cultures that it conquered. Even 1,500 years after the fall of Rome, its legacy survives in the languages, architecture, laws and thinking of today. Ancient Roman civilization is still regarded as one of the great ages of humankind.

At the time that ancient Rome was beginning to expand its territories, many Mediterranean countries were made up of farming communities. In neighbouring Greece there was an advanced culture, but the Greeks wasted a lot of time on civil wars. They had never colonized the other lands around them, apart from some colonies in southern Italy. Other peoples, like the Etruscans, were exploring new lands; settling in the plains of Italy, north and south of the River Tiber. It was Rome, however, that became the most important city in Italy.

▼ This map shows Italy in the early days of Rome, around 750 BC. It was inhabited by immigrants from Greece, North Africa and Europe. Rome was just one of many small settlements and yet it was Rome that eventually dominated the area.

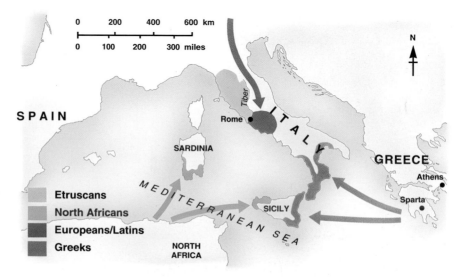

Etruscans
North Africans
Europeans/Latins
Greeks

SPAIN
Rome
SARDINIA
ITALY
GREECE
Athens
Sparta
SICILY
MEDITERRANEAN SEA
NORTH AFRICA
Tiber

0   200   400   600 km
0   100   200   300 miles

N

Italy is in the centre of the Mediterranean; it has a long coastline, making links with Greece, Africa and Spain possible by sea. This put Italy in a central position to develop trade in the region. Rome itself was in the fertile valley of the River Tiber, in a warm climate. Inland it was easy to defend, with the natural defences of the seven hills, but at the same time the river gave it access to the sea for war and trading. Much of the rest of Italy is mountainous. All around Rome were other peoples who wanted more land, so at first Rome only went to war to defend its land. Rome first drove other competing cultures out of Italy, made peace with the conquered tribes and then set out to destroy their competitors further afield.

▼ This was the centre of the Roman Empire – the Forum in Rome. The three pillars are the remains of the temple to Castor and Pollux, while behind it is the *Curia* where the Roman senate met.

Legends and Origins

The story of ancient Rome began around 800 BC, in a small settlement on one of the seven hills of Rome; but historians do not know how, or exactly when, this first settlement developed.

In one legend, there was a king called Numitor. His sons were killed by his jealous brother, Amulius, who then made Numitor's daughter, Rhea Silvia, become a priestess. After Mars, the god of war, fell in love with her, Rhea had twin sons, Romulus and Remus. When Amulius found out, he threw Rhea and her babies into the River Tiber. A female wolf found the twins and brought them up. Years later, a shepherd discovered them and brought them to Numitor, where the whole story was explained.

Amulius was killed in battle, so the twins decided to build a new city to celebrate his death. An oracle told them to build the city on the Palatine Hill; it also said that Romulus was to be the king of the city. Romulus took a plough and ploughed a line to show the city's boundaries. Remus, now jealous of his brother, jumped over the furrow to disobey his brother and Romulus killed him. Romulus then became the first king of Rome.

▼ In *The Early History of Rome* Livy writes: 'A she-wolf, coming down from the neighbouring hills...heard the children...she treated them with such gentleness that Faustulus, the king's herdsman found her licking them with her tongue.'

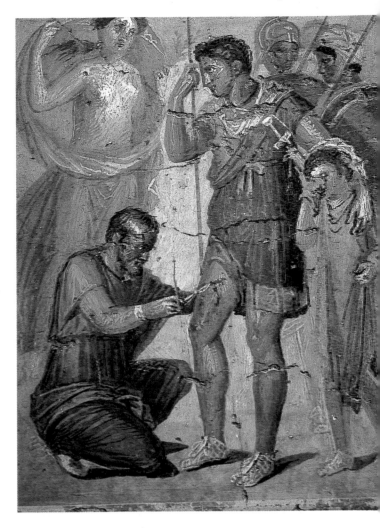

▶ In this fresco from Pompeii we see Aeneas, the ancestor of Romulus and Remus, having his wounds dressed after the terrible battle at Troy.

Historians know that the first people to live on the Palatine Hill were Latin peoples from northern Italy. They lived in small oblong huts made of wooden poles, woven around with twigs and branches and filled in with clay. They herded sheep and cattle and kept goats and pigs. Their burial ground was at the foot of the Palatine hill. Each of the seven hills of Rome would have been a separate village. In the very early history of Rome, these Latin people were invaded by Etruscans from the north, who became their kings. They united the seven hills into one city and also brought their skills as builders and artists to the new city.

Another legend says that a famous warrior from Troy, Aeneas, was the ancestor of Romulus and Remus. Having escaped from the ruins of the defeated city of Troy, Aeneas travelled on and sailed around the world having many adventures. Eventually he arrived in Italy and settled there. His story is told in the Aeneid, *a famous Roman poem written by Virgil. Here is a part of the story where he first sees Rome: 'Now Aeneas, looking out from the glassy ocean, sees a vast stretch of forest. The River Tiber's pleasant stream flows through it before bursting into the sea in swirling eddies. Above and all around different birds sweeten the air with song. Having ordered his companions to change course and steer for land Aeneas is elated as he makes the river's shade.'*

The Seven Kings

Romulus was said to be the first king of Rome in 753 BC. He was followed by six more kings, until 510 BC when Rome became a Republic. These kings began to make Rome an important city. First, they expanded their lands to take in a neighbouring city, Alba Longa. Then the sixth king, Servius Tullius, made Rome into a religious centre by building a shrine to Diana the hunter goddess. His son, Tarquinius Superbus, built a huge temple to Jupiter, the king of the gods. Rome soon became an important religious site.

The kings of Rome were very powerful people. They were in charge of war, public buildings and religion. They also acted as city judges. Everywhere they went, their assistants carried a bundle of rods with an axe in the middle, known as *fasces*, to show that the king had the power to have anyone executed or beaten. Servius Tullius was the first Roman king to have coins made. Before this, cows had been used as money; one cow was equal to ten sheep. Later, for convenience, people began to use bronze bars as money. Finally, a standard bronze coin stamped with a cow's head became the currency.

1084.—Roman Lictor.

▲ The kings of Rome were accompanied by a servant, called a lictor, who carried the symbols of power, the bundle of rods and an axe, the *fasces*.

It is thought that the Etruscans first came to Italy from the east, from what is now Turkey, and that they were very influenced by the Greeks, with whom they traded. At the height of their civilization they ruled nearly all of Italy, and they made an important contribution to the history of Rome. Examples of their art and technology show them to be a talented and creative people; but their separate identity was gradually lost as Rome grew more important. Historians are still unable to translate the examples of their writing that survive.

The kings also commissioned Rome's famous system of sewers. At first they had used the streams that ran between the seven hills of the city to carry waste water away, but then they began to build huge underground sewers.

However, the kings became too ruthless. The last king of all, Tarquinius Superbus, forced the citizens to give up their jobs to work for him. A later Roman historian tells the story:

'The poor were set to work in return for a miserable ration of grain: quarrying stone, cutting timber, leading the wagons, or even themselves carrying the materials on their backs. Various craftsmen, coppersmiths, carpenters and stonemasons were all forcibly removed from their private business to labour for the public good.'

A group of noblemen led a rebellion, and Tarquinius, the last Etruscan king of Rome, had to escape from the city with his supporters. The exact year of this event is not known, but it is believed to be around 510 BC. The people, having got rid of their kings, set up a republic, meaning 'rule by the people', which was headed by two consuls each year.

▶ This bronze jug from the fourth century BC shows the skilled craftsmanship of the people of the Etruscan Empire.

9

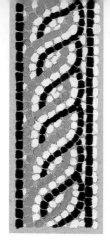

CHAPTER 2

Republic to Empire

▼ A bronze statue of a Gaulish warrior from the Imperial Period of Rome's history. His ancestors overran Rome in 386 BC.

The Republic

After 510 BC the Romans set up a new government based on wealth. At the head of the government were two consuls; they were elected by wealthy men from the senate for periods of one year. The senate was elected from the richest and most important men and its job was to advise the two consuls. The poor were called the *plebeians* and at first they had no say in government. But in 490 BC they held a protest on one of the small hills outside Rome. The leaders of Rome needed the *plebeians* to fight in their armies, so they had to agree to give them some power. They allowed them to elect two representatives, called tribunes, to speak for them. These tribunes became very powerful and could stop laws being passed if they disagreed with them. Later, the number of tribunes was increased to ten, and the *plebeians* were allowed to stand for other government jobs. After 367 BC, a consul was elected from among the *plebeians,* rather than from the wealthier classes.

Meanwhile, other cities in Italy were forming alliances against Rome.

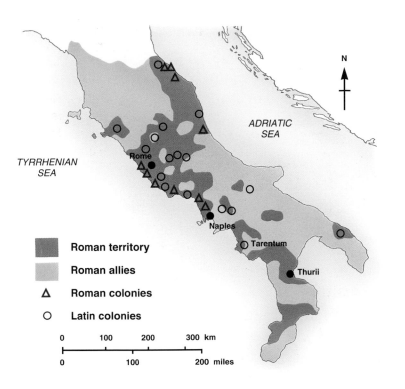

▲ This map shows how far Roman territory had expanded by about 264 BC.

Map legend:
- Roman territory
- Roman allies
- △ Roman colonies
- ○ Latin colonies

TYRRHENIAN SEA

ADRIATIC SEA

N

Rome
Naples
Tarentum
Thurii

0 100 200 300 km

0 100 200 miles

In 496 BC Rome was attacked and forced to join an alliance of Latin cities. Gradually Rome took over that alliance. Then in 386 BC, the Gauls, from northern Europe, attacked and destroyed Rome; after their victory, they stayed in Rome for a few months. In the end, the Romans had to pay the Gauls in gold to persuade them to leave the city.

The Romans rebuilt their city and constructed a strong wall around the seven hills. It was at this time that they began wars against other cities in Italy. The first of these was against the people who had once ruled them, the Etruscans.

Rome gradually captured more territory and built up an empire; by 264 BC it dominated Italy. In some cities they allowed the citizens to become Romans. Often citizens had to give up some of their land for Roman settlers to live on. Many cities were allowed to trade with Rome, but they were not allowed to trade with anyone else. Sometimes citizens from captured territories could even marry Romans. All of these territories had to supply soldiers for Rome's army.

In 451 BC a committee drew up a set of laws for the city. The laws were written on 12 bronze plaques and displayed in the city centre. They remained the law throughout the history of the Roman Empire. They covered many aspects of life, and everyone had to obey them. They laid down the punishments for murder, prohibited cremations within the city, dictated the width of roads, allowed fathers to kill their deformed children and many more things.

War Against Carthage

In the north of Africa, another great city was flourishing. Carthage had colonies all over the Mediterranean, and using its fleet of warships it traded deep into Africa, and even as far as Britain. Whenever the Carthaginians came across Roman boats they rammed into them and sank them.

In 264 BC, war broke out between Carthage and Rome on the island of Sicily. Although it started over a fairly petty incident, it was the first in a series of wars which propelled Rome into a position of great power. The Carthaginians occupied a small trading post on Sicily which the Romans attacked and drove them out from; this enraged the rulers of Carthage. A war at sea began between Rome and Carthage, with the Romans having to build ships quickly to match the might of the Carthaginian fleet. The Roman boats had a sharp spike on the front which was let down before ramming the Carthaginian boat, locking them together and allowing troops to rush aboard the enemy ship. In 241 BC, the Romans won the first war; they then invaded Carthaginian colonies in Corsica and Sardinia.

▲ This terracotta plaque shows a war elephant like those used by Hannibal in his trip across the Alps. One of their most useful functions was to frighten the local tribes who were too afraid to attack such huge creatures.

▼ This mosaic shows a Roman warship. These ships would have an underwater ram, used for breaking holes in the enemy's ships. The eye of Osiris on the front of the boat was to ward off disease.

▶ In 204 BC the Roman general, Scipio, invaded Africa and met Hannibal in battle. Scipio defeated Hannibal, and the Carthaginian leader was recalled to defend his homeland. Scipio was given the name 'Africanus', as a reward for his great victory.

In 218 BC a second war broke out, this time involving the famous Carthaginian general, Hannibal, who led his troops from Spain over the Alps to Italy. Hannibal's troops travelled to an area south of Rome, where they were based for 14 years and where they engaged in many wars with Roman troops. In 202 BC Hannibal took his troops back to Africa to defend Carthage against Roman troops. He was defeated at the battle of Zama, and Carthage surrendered. Rome gave the Carthaginians a restricted area of territory, made them surrender most of their ships and armour and imposed a heavy fine on them. Carthage was now much less powerful as an empire and yet still the Romans were not satisfied. They began a third war with Carthage in 149 BC and this time they did not stop until the entire city was destroyed. Some stories say that they even sowed the fields of Carthage with salt, making them useless for agriculture. The 50,000 survivors in the city were sold as slaves.

Hannibal became a general at the age of 26. He knew that Rome had hundreds of ships and could easily beat him at sea, so he decided to force the Romans to fight on land. He marched his troops to the north of Spain, into France and through the majestic Italian Alps into Italy. He had 100,000 troops and 36 elephants. By midsummer he was in France; but he had lost 40,000 men fighting against the tribes of Spain and France. Once he even had to blast his way through a rock wall by heating the rocks and then throwing cold wine on to them in order to crack them. By the time Hannibal reached northern Italy he had only 26,000 men left. Despite this, he still managed to twice defeat Roman armies. After Hannibal was called back to Carthage and defeated, he went into exile and spent the rest of his life as a hunted man.

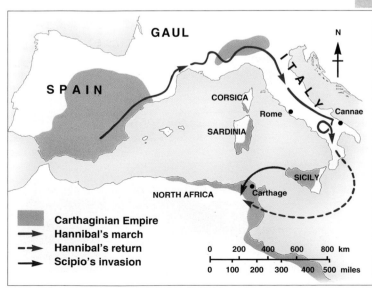

GAUL

N

SPAIN

CORSICA

Rome

Cannae

ITALY

SARDINIA

SICILY

NORTH AFRICA

Carthage

- Carthaginian Empire
- → Hannibal's march
- --▶ Hannibal's return
- → Scipio's invasion

| 0 | 200 | 400 | 600 | 800 km |
| 0 | 100 | 200 | 300 | 400 | 500 miles |

The Civil Wars

In the 100 years following Hannibal's defeat, the Romans expanded their Empire until it covered much of the land bordering the Mediterranean. The Empire was ruled over by governors who grew very rich.

Back in Rome, wealthy soldiers began to spend lots of money bribing people to vote them into power. On the other hand, peasants who had fought in the wars against Carthage returned to find that their farms were ruined. The wealthy people bought up the farms and sent their slaves to work on them, while the homeless peasants drifted into Rome to find work. They became very discontented and, in 133 BC, a tribune called Tiberius Gracchus suggested that the big farms be broken up and given back to the poor. The land owners and senators did not like this and started riots. Other plans to give out land to the poor were also stopped.

The poor people finally began to vote for consuls who would help them and oppose the powerful men of the senate. Civil war broke out in Rome in 88 BC and the senators took away the power of the tribunes.

Pompey first became consul in 70 BC. In between his years as consul he was a very successful general and won a lot of land for Rome; he also mounted a successful campaign against the pirates who were robbing Roman ships in the Mediterranean. He married Julius Caesar's daughter, Julia, but she died in childbirth five years later. One Roman writer, Lucan, suggested that if she had lived Caesar and Pompey might have stayed friends rather than become enemies:

'Julia alone, if granted by the fates a longer life, could have restrained her resentful husband and her father too; could have pushed aside their swords and joined the hands that held the weapons...Her death shattered family ties and released the enmity between the two.'

In 62 BC a general called Pompey was made consul and he restored the power of the tribunes. Another general at this time was Julius Caesar. In 51 BC, after a series of successful campaigns there, Caesar was given command of Gaul. For a while these two men, with the help of a third, called Crassus, ruled Rome between them as consuls. They were known as the Triumvirate. Eventually, Crassus was murdered and Caesar decided to take power for himself. Caesar, still in charge of the territory of Gaul, was a very successful general and a great leader. He was popular with the poor, who supported him in politics. Pompey had the support of the senators.

In 49 BC Caesar marched with his troops into Rome. Pompey and the senators withdrew to Greece, where they intended to plan a campaign against Caesar. But Caesar caught them, defeated Pompey and chased him to Egypt. Before Caesar could take Pompey prisoner, his one-time friend was murdered by the Egyptians. Caesar stayed in Egypt, settling his affairs, until 45 BC when he returned to Rome to take power.

▼ Julius Caesar became sole ruler of Rome and people began to fear his power. He was stabbed to death in 44 BC by conspirators.

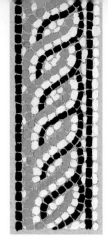

CHAPTER 3

The Roman Empire

The Emperors

Julius Caesar was a particularly popular leader with the poorer people of Rome. He ordered marshland to be drained for the poor people to farm, and arranged for others to get land in Rome's colonies. He also invented the Julian calendar, the predecessor of our modern calendar. But he had many enemies among the rich and powerful, and only five months after he had come to Rome he was murdered.

Caesar's nephew, Octavian, had to fight and defeat Mark Antony, who had been Julius Caesar's co-consul, before he could take on leadership of Rome. From then onwards, Octavian called himself Augustus Caesar. He was emperor until he died in AD 14. It was under him that Rome became an empire; he still called the Empire a republic, but he kept all the real powers of state for himself. He was a good ruler who improved the city, reorganized the army and chose good governors for the Roman colonies. He had hundreds of miles of roads built to improve both trade and communications.

▲ A bronze head of the Emperor Claudius, found at Saxmundham in England. He was a good ruler but he often drifted off into day-dreams while carrying out his official duties.

Probably the worst emperor was Nero. At first he was so inexperienced that he wanted to abolish all taxes, so that people would like him. Later he made several attempts to have his mother killed and he had two of his wives killed. He created two new public festivals at which everyone had to listen to him play and sing. Eventually the senate declared Nero a public enemy and Nero killed himself.

For 20 years after Augustus became emperor, the Empire was at peace and people settled down to build new cities. When he died he was made into a god.

Since the emperor was not a king and the title was not hereditary, anyone who had support from important people could come to power. The men who became emperors after Augustus were both good and bad. Caligula was so power-crazed that he made his horse a consul and built a marble stable for it. Claudius (who was found hiding behind a curtain in the imperial palace after the murder of Caligula and proclaimed emperor) developed into a serious and steady ruler. He expanded the civil service and increased the powers of imperial governors abroad. In AD 43 he conquered Britain, and even allowed important non-Romans across the Empire to become Roman citizens. He died in suspicious circumstances in AD 54, after eating poisonous mushrooms.

After this there were many emperors; in one year, AD 69, there were four different emperors, three of whom were either assassinated or committed suicide. In AD 117 Hadrian became emperor. He was Spanish and was a brilliant general. He worked hard to improve the Empire and not just expand it.

There were 66 emperors of Rome in all; the lengths of their reigns vary from 41 years to six months.

▼ This statue shows Caligula and his horse. In three years Caligula wasted all the savings of his predecessor, Tiberius. For the first time in Roman history he imposed taxes on the sale of food, a very unpopular measure.

Expanding the Empire

From the time of the emperor Augustus, the Roman Empire was rapidly expanding. Anybody who wanted a job in the government in Rome had to prove their strength. They had to do this by conquering new territories or stopping a rebellion in one of the colonies. Many of the Roman emperors added to the size of the Empire during their reigns by conquering new land.

Julius Caesar had invaded Britain twice, in 55 and 54 BC, and while he was governor of Gaul from 58 to 49 BC, he expanded Rome's territory to cover all of modern France.

In 31 BC, Augustus, Caesar's adopted son, seized Egypt; the country had previously been an ally, but not part of the Empire. He also expanded the Empire in Europe, along the River Rhine and the River Danube, and stopped rebellions in parts of Spain and the Alps. Claudius, who ruled from AD 41 to 54, personally led a successful invasion of Britain. He also annexed Mauretania, in north Africa, and Thrace, along the shore of the Black Sea.

In AD 70, under the emperor Vespasian, Jerusalem was attacked and made part of the Empire. The Empire grew to its biggest ever, between AD 98-117, under the rule of Trajan. He sent his troops into large areas of the Middle East and modern Romania.

So, by 117 AD, the Roman Empire covered the whole coastline of north Africa, from Egypt to modern Morocco; all of Europe as far north as the River Danube, England and Wales; modern Israel, and the Middle East as far east as the Rivers Tigris and Euphrates.

▼ At Hadrian's wall, the outsides of the wall were stone banks. They were ten feet apart and filled with rubble and mortar. It was topped with battlements and a walkway for sentries.

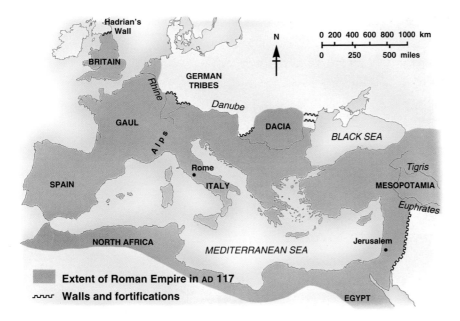

◀ In AD 117 the Roman Empire had reached its greatest extent. Where there were no natural boundaries, walls were built to mark the outer limits of the empire.

The borders of the Empire stopped at natural barriers, such as the rivers of Europe, and the deserts of the Middle East. Where there was no natural boundary, in Britain and Germany, border walls were built to mark off conquered territories. The best example of a Roman border wall is Hadrian's Wall in England, which was the project of the Emperor Hadrian. It became obvious that Scotland would be too expensive to conquer, so Hadrian ordered that a 6 metre-high stone and turf wall be built across England, from the east coast to the west, about 117 km in length.

Sixteen large forts were built into the wall at regular intervals. Inside each fort lived between 500 and 1,000 soldiers. There were also 80 fortlets called milecastles, which held between eight and 32 men, and lots of watchtowers which could hold a few sentries. The towers, forts and milecastles may have signalled to each other.

At Vindolanda, a Roman fort near Hadrian's wall, a message, thought to be military intelligence, was found: '...the Britons are unprotected by armour. There are very many cavalry. The cavalry do not use swords nor do the wretched Britons take up fixed positions in order to throw javelins...'.

19

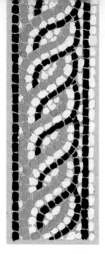

CHAPTER 4

Politics and Society

Government and Law

In the Roman Republic the government was headed by two consuls who made the laws. They had absolute power, but either could challenge the acts of the other, and they both had to agree for a change in the law to be accepted. They were advised by the senate, which was originally made up only of rich men; these were the *patres*, or 'fathers' of the community. Representatives of the ordinary people, called tribunes, could block any measure proposed by a member of the senate. There were also two elected assemblies made up of the ordinary citizens of Rome; in theory these Roman citizens had an equal say in what went on in Rome, but in reality the assembly was controlled by the senate.

When the Emperor Augustus came to power in 27 BC he changed this system. There were still two consuls and a senate, but they could not pass laws – only the emperor could do that. The emperor had taken on the power of a consul, a tribune and chief priest. He did not call himself Emperor, but chose the title 'first citizen'.

▼ These are the remains of the Basilica Aemilia in Rome. It was built in AD 179 by Aemilius Lepidus the censor. Basilicas were the public halls which lined Rome's forums or public squares. They were used for meetings or as shops and markets.

This title gave him the right to speak first at senate meetings. Once he had said what he thought no-one dared to disagree, because Augustus had absolute power. He also chose all the senators and consuls. The assembly still met, but its job was to choose judges and agree to Augustus' laws; it was no longer a very powerful body. Every emperor after Augustus kept up this system of government.

The Twelve Tablets, which had been written in 451 BC, were still in use in imperial times, but many more laws had been added to them. In the second century AD, the Emperor Hadrian decided that laws should be exactly the same all over the Roman Empire; so he ordered a lawyer to collect and write down all the laws. If a Roman citizen in Britain, Africa or any other colony thought he had been mistreated in a courtroom in his own country, he could go to Rome to appeal against the ruling. Juries decided if someone was innocent or guilty. Sometimes a jury could have as many as 75 people.

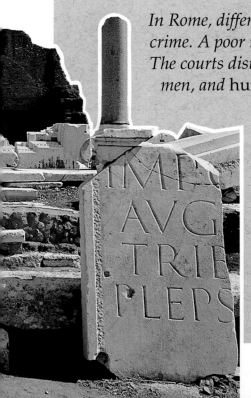

In Rome, different people were punished in different ways for the same crime. A poor man would get a harsher punishment than a rich one. The courts distinguished between honestiores, *wealthy or upper class men, and* humiliores, *or poor men. A slave would nearly always get the worst punishment. No-one went to prison in Roman society. For small crimes they paid fines, but for serious crimes they were banished or had their property taken away from them. If someone was sentenced to death they were executed by crucifixion. Poor people were sent to the public games, and died fighting a wild animal or another slave. The death sentence could be imposed for stealing crops or speaking unfairly about somebody, as well as for murder.*

▼ This pavement mosaic from Ostia, the port of Rome, shows a man loading a merchant ship with *amphorae*. These pottery vessels would carry wine or oil. One of these ships could carry 6,000 or more *amphorae*. The ships varied in size from 18 m long to 30 m long.

Trade

Trade was very important to the Roman Empire. The city of Rome produced very little of the basic things it needed, such as food, and so it had to be imported from the colonies. Corn was the most important and biggest import and it was brought in from all over the Empire: from North Africa, Spain, France, Britain and the Middle East. Slaves were another very important product and were also imported from all over the Empire. From Egypt came papyrus writing paper and from Dacia (modern Romania), Spain and Britain came gold and silver. Glass came from Egypt and linen cloth came from Arabia. Wine came from Gaul (modern France) and Spain. From Britain came delicacies like shellfish. Wild animals for the public shows and games came from Africa.

Rome also traded with countries that were not part of the Empire, such as Poland which traded amber, or modern Georgia which traded cattle. Silk came from China, and spices, jewels and perfumes came from India. From across the deserts goods arrived at the Roman colonies on camel trains. The enormous network of roads carried wagons, loaded with goods, as far as the coasts; then trading ships, called *corbitae*, brought the goods across the sea. *Corbitae* were big, slow-moving ships and often had a huge, carved goose's head on the prow. The goose was the symbol of the goddess Isis, who was believed to protect sailors. Each ship had one big square mainsail, and a smaller one at the front which was used to steer.

Pirates were a serious problem to Roman traders. In 67 BC, ships in the Mediterranean were facing constant attacks. Pirates would board merchant ships and take their goods. Sailors who were citizens of the Roman Empire would be dressed up in Roman clothes and made to walk the plank; important rich men would be held to ransom. When the consul Pompey was a general, he was sent to rid the sea of the pirates. He was given 250 ships, 100,000 soldiers and 4,000 cavalry. Within three months he had taken thousands of prisoners and put all the pirates out of business.

Ships sailed between March and November when there was less risk of storms at sea. At the mouths of major harbours, the Romans built lighthouses with fires burning at the top. When the ships arrived at the big Roman port of Ostia the goods were unloaded onto flat-bottomed barges and carried up the River Tiber, to Rome.

▼ This map shows the main trade routes used when the Roman Empire was at its height. Goods were carried from all corners of the Empire and beyond, to Rome.

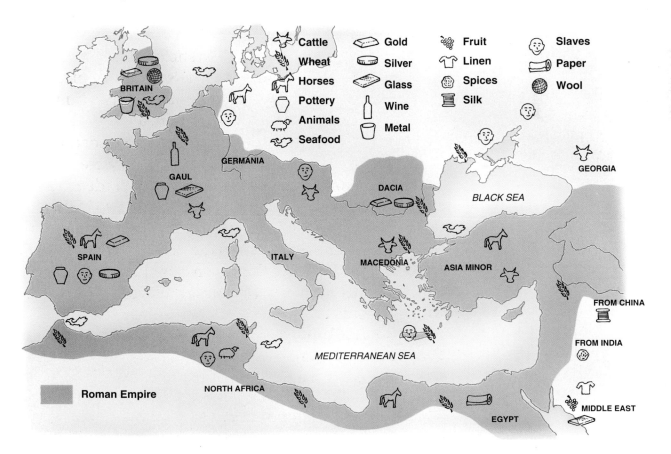

Cattle • Wheat • Horses • Pottery • Animals • Seafood
Gold • Silver • Glass • Wine • Metal
Fruit • Linen • Spices • Silk
Slaves • Paper • Wool

BRITAIN

GERMANIA

GAUL

GEORGIA

DACIA

BLACK SEA

SPAIN

ITALY

MACEDONIA

ASIA MINOR

FROM CHINA

FROM INDIA

MEDITERRANEAN SEA

Roman Empire

NORTH AFRICA

MIDDLE EAST

EGYPT

The Army

Rome had a very efficient army. In the early days of the Republic all men were called up in the event of an emergency. They left their job for a few days while the war was on and then went home – if they survived. Later, when the Empire was big, the army had professional soldiers.

The professional Roman soldier went through a lengthy training session before he was ready to fight. He was trained in marching, riding, building a camp, stone slinging and swimming. Weapons training was very important. Recruits practised with heavy wooden swords and cane shields. They were also trained to throw wooden spears.

After training the soldier joined a legion. Legionaries were divided into four types of fighters. In battle the poorest soldiers, the *velites*, fought single handedly. They had no body armour and carried a light spear and shield. At the front of the battle line were the *hastati*. They wore light armour and carried a sword and two javelins. Behind them were the *principes*, who had swords, spears and cylinder-shaped shields. At the back of the battle line were sword fighters called *triarii*. These were the most experienced soldiers and had spears and full body armour. They rarely fought because the ranks in front of them did most of the work.

▼ This relief carving shows Roman soldiers in the battle against the Barbarians. They are cavalrymen and so come from the wealthier Roman classes or are allies of the Romans.

▶ The Praetorian Guard was a 900 strong army. The Guard was created by the Emperor Augustus. They became very powerful, often choosing the next emperor in times of crisis. Behind them is their legionary standard – an eagle holding a thunderbolt in its claws.

At Vindolanda (modern Chesterholm), a fort near Hadrian's Wall in England, a tiny scrap of a letter from home has been found. It says: 'I have sent you... pairs of woollen socks, two pairs of sandals and two pairs of underpants.' On the cold border those things must have been very useful.

At the flanks of the battle line were the cavalry. The Romans used cavalrymen, supplied by the local allies, wherever they were fighting. They wore full body armour and a helmet. In Hadrian's time the horses also wore armour. A Roman legionary soldier joined up for 20 years. He was well paid and got bonuses if the army won a big victory. But his life was hard. He had to buy his own weapons, food and clothes.

He had to march up to 30 km a day. He carried a pack weighing about 30 kg, including two huge stakes, which were used to build a defensive wall when the army made camp. At the end of the day's march he had to help build the camp for the night. He carried three days' supply of rations, made up of wholemeal biscuits, bacon, cheese and wine. When they were stationed on the frontiers life got a little easier, with better food and even a chance to start a family with a local girl.

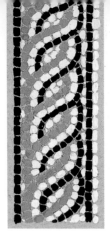

CHAPTER 5

Ruling the Empire

As the Romans conquered more countries they needed to make the people of those countries happy to be under Roman rule. Most of the countries they invaded consisted of small villages with basic technology. At first, the Romans built forts to control the local people, who might have been restless after being invaded. A fort contained barracks for the troops, houses for officers, workshops, granaries and a hospital.

When a legionary retired after his 20 years of service, he was often given land near the fort where he could build his house. In this way towns developed around the forts. Roman engineers and architects built beautiful buildings, put in plumbing and built aqueducts, temples and wide roads. After the local people had got used to the Romans they often preferred the protection and amenities of town life to living in small isolated communities. In exchange for all these benefits, the people of the provinces paid taxes to support the army and pay tribute to Rome.

▲ In this Roman classroom the bearded figure in the middle is the teacher; either side of him are his pupils. To the right is a slave, holding his young master's schoolbag. These boys learned to read and write in Latin.

All over the Empire, citizens paid taxes to Rome in exchange for protection and law and order. People paid taxes on the value of their homes and farms each year. Travelling tax inspectors visited every farm and house throughout the Empire to decide how much they had to pay. Where soldiers were stationed in a town or village, the local people paid another type of tax in actual food for the soldiers. Thirdly, as in many modern countries, the Romans also paid tax on the goods they bought and sold and on any wealth that they inherited. At the height of the Empire this system ran well and was quite fair, but by the fourth century AD the cost of running the Empire and paying for the endless wars had become very high. This led to tax increases and the burden that they created added to the civil unrest all over the Empire.

At first the provinces traded their raw materials, such as metal, wood and crops, for Roman manufactured goods like pottery. Later they built their own workshops and ports and became trading centres in their own right. Eventually Rome bought more things from the provinces than it exported to them.

But the Romans did not just export their own culture. In return, the cultures that they conquered were brought to Rome in the form of architecture, literature and religion. The Republic copied its boats from the Carthaginians and their enthusiasm for the Greek language was proved by the fact that the emperor Hadrian was said to have been more fluent in Greek than in Latin. Most of the slaves that taught young Roman boys were Greek. Even some of the religions of the people that they conquered were taken back to Rome and became very popular.

▶ Roman architects and engineers travelled to all quarters of the empire. These are the remains of the forum in the Roman city at Sufetula in North Africa.

The Social Ladder

Everyone had a place on the social ladder in Roman society. Of the million people who lived in Rome during the first century AD, most men were citizens and, as such, had rights and duties laid down by law. But not all citizens were equal. Every five years a census was taken in Rome and men were assessed as to their status. There were three main classes of citizen. At the very top were the *nobiles* who were the richest men and who were born into noble families. At first only these men could become senators, but later any wealthy man who had proved himself to be a good citizen could be a senator. Below them were the *equites*, who were less wealthy and who were often businessmen. They could become magistrates. The third order of citizenship was the *plebeians*.

There was a way for slaves to win their freedom; under the Empire it became quite fashionable for wealthy men to free their slaves after a certain time, or when the slave had saved enough money to buy his freedom. Then the slave became a freedman and any children he had after that time became full Roman citizens. So, in theory, it would even be possible for these children to become senators when they grew up.

The *plebeians* were the ordinary men of the city, such as shopkeepers, craftsmen and agricultural workers.

There were millions of other people in the Roman Empire who were not included in these levels of citizenship. For example, women and children only had rights because they belonged to their husband or father. People who lived in the Roman provinces had varying degrees of citizenship. In some provinces they were equal citizens, but could not become *nobiles* or *equites*. In other provinces they could; Trajan and Hadrian, both from Spain, rose to the position of emperor. In other provinces, they had citizenship rights as regards trade and intermarriage, but could not vote; and in others still, their citizenship was limited to paying taxes and providing men for the army.

In the worst position of all were the slaves. They were seen merely as possessions, owned entirely by their masters, who could do whatever they wanted to them. Varro, a writer from the first century AD, called slaves 'a species of articulate farming stock', which was his way of saying that they were like farm animals that could speak. Most of the hard labour in Rome was carried out by slaves.

▼ Two household slaves go about their daily routine. Slaves worked on farms, in mines and factories, and on building sites. They maintained the water supply, worked as clerks, teachers, actors, doctors and artists.

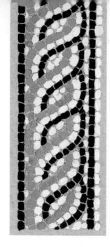

CHAPTER 6

Religion in Rome

▼ Sacrifices to Mars were usually a pig, sheep and an ox, but on October 15th every year the winning male racehorse at the Circus Maximus was slaughtered in Mars' honour.

Gods and Goddesses

Ancient Rome had many magnificent temples dedicated to the huge family of gods in the state religion. Jupiter, who represented justice and honour, was the most powerful. His brothers were Dis, the god of the underworld, and Neptune, the god of the sea. His sisters , Vesta and Ceres, were responsible for the hearth and agriculture, while his wife Juno protected women and childbirth. Jupiter's children were Vulcan the god of craftsmen and Mars, who was the god of war and the father of Romulus and Remus. Diana was the goddess of hunters, and her sister, Minerva, was the goddess of crafts and wisdom. Mercury was the god of trade and Bacchus was the god of wine. The god of prophecy and healing was Apollo.

Each god could be asked for help by performing a sacrifice at their temple. The temples were guarded by priests and priestesses who also conducted the ceremonies. The Romans believed that sacrifices were very important to the gods. If something went wrong during the ceremony, it had to be done all over again.

Two household gods, called Lares, hold up horns showing the bounty of the fields, while the household *genius*, believed to be the life force of the head of the household, stands between them.

Bulls, sheep and pigs were often sacrificed, and their organs were inspected for signs that would show whether or not the gods were pleased.

The Romans believed that there were spirits all around them. A rock or a stream or even a door had its own spirit. In the home, Janus, who had two heads (and gave his name to the first month of the year), was the god who guarded the door, while other gods called the *penates* guarded the larder. Also in the house were the spirits of dead ancestors. Tiny statues of them were kept in a cupboard and worshipped.

The Romans believed that priests could tell what was going to happen in the future by examining the insides of the animals that they sacrificed. There were also prophets who looked into the future by examining the sky, birds in flight, cloud formations and lightning. In times of national emergency a very special set of books, written by a prophetess called the Sybil, could be consulted. Before any battle, the generals always consulted some special hens which had been blessed by a priest. They were given corn, and if they refused to eat the battle would be lost. The writer Suetonius tells the story of one general who ignored the warning: 'He began a sea battle though the sacred chickens had refused to eat. In contempt of religious practices he threw the chickens into the sea, remarking that if they did not eat they could drink.' He recalls that the general lost 93 ships and their crews in that battle, and barely escaped with his own life.

Foreign Religions

The Romans tolerated other religions in their city. As foreigners came and settled in Rome they brought their religions with them, and the government was generally happy to allow this.

One imported goddess was Cybele, the Great Mother. She was a very popular goddess with women and she was believed to help them in childbirth and with their general health. The religion originally came from Asia Minor (modern Turkey) in about 204 BC. The ceremonies included dancing and sacrifices and to make up for sins they had committed, women were often sent to bathe in the freezing River Tiber, or to a distant temple to bring back holy water.

Isis was another imported goddess, this time from Egypt. She was ruler of all heaven and earth. Another new religion was popularized when the Egyptian Queen Cleopatra visited Rome in 45 BC. This cult celebrated the death and rebirth of the consort of Isis, a young man called Osiris.

The Romans first came across Judaism when they invaded Palestine in 63 BC, and at first the religion was tolerated. The Emperor Augustus even decreed that Jews did not have to appear in court on their Sabbath. Jews came to Rome to live and many Romans were converted to Judaism. But their religion said that they could only worship one god, and the Romans wanted to put statues of their divine emperors into the synagogues. The Jews refused and Judaism was eventually banned in Rome.

▲ A head of the Persian god Mithras. Mithras was originally a sun god. In the initiation ceremony his worshippers were baptised in the blood of a bull. Sinners were punished in the afterlife by hell fire.

Christianity was also tolerated at first in Rome. Their religion forbade the worship of any other god and, like the Jews, they would not accept statues of the emperors in their places of worship. The Romans then banned Christianity and began a long campaign against the Christians. The Emperor Nero was especially cruel to them, accusing them of starting the great fire in AD 64 and having many of them thrown to the lions at the games. But the situation was to change. Later emperors tolerated Christianity as the religion spread; in AD 391 it was even declared the state religion, and Rome became the centre of Christianity.

▶ The cult of Isis was brought to the Roman Empire in the first century AD. It was the first religion in the empire to worship a single deity, the goddess Isis.

Mithraism originated in India and Persia. The cult worshipped just one god, Mithras. Unlike the often violent gods of the Romans, Mithras was a god who encouraged forgiveness, kindness and respect. The religion was very popular with soldiers, especially around the Empire's borders, and for a time it was the main rival of Christianity. Worshippers of Mithras believed in life after death, and that all men were equal (women were not allowed to worship Mithras). Joining the religion involved undergoing initiation rites and learning the secrets of the religion. Mithras is represented as a man slaying a bull.

CHAPTER 7

Art, Literature and Technology

Architecture and Decoration

If you could go back in time to a Roman city, you would probably be amazed by the size and beauty of public buildings such as temples, public baths and theatres. The Romans were able to build such huge and ornate buildings for three reasons. Firstly, they learnt how to build arches and vaults from the Etruscans. This allowed them to construct large round roofs, long bridges and aqueducts. Secondly, from the Greeks they copied the rows of pillars which supported and decorated the roofs of the buildings. And finally, they had their own invention – concrete. This allowed them to build much bigger structures than would be possible with just stone blocks and mortar.

▼ In the inaugural festival for the Colosseum, or Amphitheatre Flavium, 100 days of continuous gladiatorial games and beast hunts took place. The stone to build it came from Tivoli, transported along a road specially built for that purpose. The three storeys of columns are in different designs while the fourth storey is a solid wall fitted with masts. These were used to pull out a huge canvas awning to keep the sun off spectators.

▶ Roman mosaics tell us a lot about Roman life. This one shows a Roman garrison detachment on the Nile. Here we can see troops amongst the lush greenery of Egypt.

The Romans loved to decorate their buildings using lots of different styles. The squares and temples were decorated with bronze and marble statues. To mark a particular victory in battle the emperors often had columns erected, showing the battle and the spoils of war. One of these, which still stands, is Trajan's Column, which was erected to commemorate his conquest of Dacia. Walls might be decorated with bas relief carvings, which were statues partly carved out of marble blocks. Another form of wall decoration was the fresco, where paint was applied to drying plaster walls. The most famous form of Roman decoration is mosaic. This is where thousands of tiny, coloured cubes are set in a pattern into a cement base. They are often seen as floor coverings or wall decorations.

The Pantheon in Rome is a typical example of Roman architecture at its grandest. It was built in 25 BC originally (as a temple), and later rebuilt around AD 124 by the Emperor Hadrian. It is a round, domed building 43 m in diameter and 43 m high. At the very top it has a hole in the roof, 8.5 m in diameter, to let in light. Its walls were covered in marble, and inside it was decorated with statues of the gods. Huge bronze doors are still in place today.

Another vast building in Rome was the Basilica Julia, which was a single hall with colonnades occupying an area of 100 m by 36 m. Roman theatres were equally huge. They were built as semicircles and their great height was made possible by a series of arches which supported the weight of the building. The most famous Roman building of all, the Colosseum, was commissioned by the Emperor Titus. It is oval in shape and 200 m long. It regularly held 45,000 spectators and was built entirely of stone, in three tiers of arches.

Technology

As we have seen, the Romans used arches and concrete in their buildings. Besides these, they had many other inventive building techniques. One of the things that they always needed to do was to bring a fresh water supply into the city. As early as the fourth century BC they did this by building aqueducts which carried water for miles. These were always on a slight slope, so that water ran downhill all the way into the city.

Aqueducts were built on arches, which needed a minimum of building materials, so that the weight of the structure did not make it unstable. By the first century AD, there were eight aqueducts providing water for the Romans, extending over 80 km. They were built over a period of hundreds of years, to keep pace with the increasing population of Rome. When the Romans had to bring water uphill they made waterwheels. Here a system of wheels, turned by slaves, brought the water up from one level to the next.

▼ The pont du Gard, at Nîmes in France, has three tiers of arches which carried a water channel 50 m above the river. It was probably built some time in the second century AD, under the rule of the Emperor Antoninus.

Their bridge-building techniques were also very clever. Firstly they put a wooden bridge over the river, supported by a series of anchored boats. Then they drove wooden stakes into the riverbed, making the frame for a pillar. The water was pumped out of this wooden frame and blocks of stone were put inside. Wooden frames were then built between the stone pillars, and stone arches built over them.

Many building techniques used by the Romans were the forerunners of a lot of the technology that we use today. They used simple wooden cranes, driven by slaves in a treadmill, to lift heavy objects. Scaffolding was also erected on the sides of buildings, for workmen to walk on. Walls were built of brick or stone. Inside walls were often wooden frames filled with rubble and covered with a surface layer of plaster. The builder's tools were also remarkably similar to those we use today. From a Roman workman's toolbag we would recognize planes, pliers, trowels and axes, as well as many other things.

▲ This illustration, from a builder's tomb, shows a Roman crane. At the bottom slaves are inside the treadmill, winding ropes in a pulley system. The crane was used to lift large stones into place.

After the water had travelled from its source in the hills to the city, it was piped into large storage tanks. From there, more pipes carried it to the city's fountains, public toilets and baths. The pipes were made of sections of lead bent into tubes and fitted together. Most people collected their water from the public fountains, although the very rich often bribed the slaves who worked on the water system, to pipe a supply into their private houses. Waste water was carried away by a series of sewer pipes. In the blocks of flats, called insulae, *there would be a pipe into which tenants could throw their waste. This flowed out into the gutter and down into the sewers. Excavated streets in Ostia or Pompeii still have stepping stones across the roads; they were there so that people did not have to walk through the waste water.*

Roman Writers

Ancient Rome produced many writers who were very influential men in their times, and whose surviving works are still very well thought of today. Some of them wrote plays which were performed in theatres all over the Roman Empire. The performances, which were free to all citizens, were paid for by rich men; they often did this hoping that the public would be grateful and would vote for them at election time. We still have 20 comedies written by Plautus. He was a poor man who worked in a bakery until he had his first play performed. His plays are very funny, with lots of slapstick comedy, and characters that the people of Rome would recognize from their daily lives, such as scheming slaves or nosy neighbours. Shakespeare used one of Plautus' stories as a model, when he wrote his play *The Comedy of Errors*. Terence was another very famous comic playwright. He began life as a slave and wrote only six plays before being killed in a shipwreck at the age of 26.

Catullus and Horace are two famous Roman poets who expressed their feelings about life and their fellow citizens in their poetry. Catullus came from quite a wealthy family. He wrote very romantic poetry to his mistress, whom he called Lesbia in his poems. Horace was the son of a freed slave.

▶ The actors in Plautus' and Terence's plays wore masks. Each type of mask represented a different type of character and would be easily recognized as that type by the audience. Other stage props included a complex system of backdrops which could be raised and lowered behind the actors. The first stone theatre was built by Pompey in AD 55. It held 27,000 people, a lot fewer than an amphitheatre would hold.

Pliny lived during the rule of Nero and Vespasian. He came from a wealthy family, and was himself an important member of the government. He is remembered for his Natural History *which is a book about the natural sciences: biology, geology and geography. He spent all his time reading or making notes on what he read. He loved to research into everything himself. In AD 79 he went to see the eruption of the volcano Vesuvius, and while trying to get close to the eruptions, he was choked to death by the fumes.*

Horace had worked as a clerk until a rich nobleman, who liked his poetry, decided to give him enough money to give up his job to write poetry. Horace wrote about everyday things: too much garlic in food, boring people and advice to the young. Ovid was also a brilliant poet; his poetry was often about Roman mythology and was very entertaining. Virgil wrote poetry about country life and the beauty of Italy. He also wrote about the glory of Rome in the *Aeneid*, the epic song about the founding of Rome. He never finished this work but, despite this, it was published on the orders of the Emperor Augustus.

One reason why we know so much about Rome is the work of the Roman historians. Julius Caesar wrote a history of his conquest of Gaul, while Livy wrote a history of Rome, starting from the arrival of Aeneas to his own day. Tacitus, a senator and governor of Asia, was also a famous historian, but unfortunately only a few of his books have survived. Most of what we know of the history of Roman Britain is from Tacitus' biography of his father-in-law, Agricola, who was governor of Britain for a time.

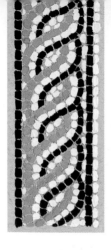

CHAPTER 8

Everyday Life

The Roman family

At the head of the Roman family was the *paterfamilias*; he was the husband and father, and the master of his slaves. Roman families were generally small, with perhaps two or three children. Newborn baby girls, or boys with birth defects, were often left to die. People wished for sons rather than daughters because only sons could inherit the family's wealth. If a family had no son, the father would adopt one. Divorce was common, and when it happened the children always stayed with their father.

In rich families the wife supervised her children's upbringing, but women from poorer families often had jobs. Women could work in shops, taverns, markets or even at the baths. A few women became doctors or lawyers, while in later times some even acted in the theatre. Roman women were often thought to be more learned than men – they were well-educated and had more spare time to study and read.

Roman children had many different kinds of toys. Girls played with rag dolls or carved stone or pottery figures and buildings; some wooden dolls with hinged arms and legs have been found. Boys played with marbles, kites, hoops and tops. They also played war games with wooden swords and shields. One popular game, called Jacks, involved each player throwing stones into the air and trying to catch them on the back of their hand. Board games were very popular in Rome. A game similar to draughts has been discovered in many places. Games of chance, such as capita et navia *(heads or tails, played with coins), and dice games were also common with both children and adults. At the Roman remains at Bath in the west of England a pair of loaded dice have been found.*

▲ These children are taking part in a religious procession. The early years were a difficult time for Roman children. If they were not abandoned at birth they still had a strong chance of dying from one of many childhood diseases.

Both boys and girls received an education in Rome. At elementary level boys and girls went, separately, to a *litterator* who taught them reading, writing and arithmetic. Once they reached 12 or 13 the girls stayed at home and had private tuition. Boys were then taught history, geography, astronomy and literature by a teacher called a *grammaticus*. Once he was 16 a boy became a citizen. From the age of 16 he could go to a *rhetor* where he was taught public speaking. Most children in Roman times were engaged at 14 or 15. The marriage ceremony was at the bride's home. After the sacrifice of an animal, friends and relatives witnessed the couple exchange vows. Following a feast at the bride's home, a procession would go to the groom's house, where the bride was carried over the threshold.

When a wealthy man died, his body would lie in state for a few days for people to pay their respects to. After that it was carried outside the city for burial or cremation, accompanied by mourners, musicians and torch bearers. A tomb would be erected to the man's memory. When people were cremated, food and clothes would be thrown onto a fire for their use in the afterlife. The poor were buried in common pits.

Daily Life

The Roman working day began at dawn with the sounds of builders and repairmen in the street, and slaves in the house. Getting out of bed and dressed was simple since both men and women slept naked and simply slipped on their garments and slippers. A wash in a basin kept them going until the afternoon when they would visit the public baths. Rich women were made up and had their hair styled by their slaves. After a simple breakfast of bread and fruit, the day's work began. Working people went off to their workplace for the day. The unemployed went as early as possible to the house of a patron (someone who was prepared to give them money and support in exchange for their loyalty).

Every morning, between 7 and 9 am, these rich men, or patrons, interviewed their clients and gave them money or advice. Children from poor families often worked alongside their parents to bring in extra money. Wealthier boys went to schools which began at dawn and lasted until noon.

Lunch for everyone was another light meal of bread, cheese, fish and vegetables. Since the working people in Rome had no kitchens, they ate at food stalls. Very poor people lived on handouts of grain and bread.

The hot Roman afternoons were dedicated to a rest, or siesta, or perhaps a visit to the baths.

▼ These Roman baths are at Bath in the west of England. Called Aquae Sulis, the baths were dedicated to the goddess Minerva and built over natural hot springs.

In the evenings people would have their main meal. This consisted of three courses, for the rich families, eaten in a formal dining room called a *triclinium*. In the room there were three couches arranged around a low table. People lay down on these couches to eat their food. The poor again bought food from food stalls. Most people went to bed by dusk because the streets of Rome were dangerous after dark; there was no street lighting and heavy traffic jammed the streets.

Every Roman city had several bath houses. They were inexpensive to visit, sometimes even free, and so were used by everyone; men on one day and women on another. The baths consisted of a series of rooms of varying temperatures, heated by a hypocaust system (see page 45). A bather gradually went from the frigidarium *(the coolest room) to the* tepidarium *and then the* caldarium *(the hottest room). Slaves were on hand to oil the skin and scrape away the day's dirt. After a wash in a hot bath the bather would return to the* frigidarium *for a cold plunge. People went to the baths to meet friends, have business meetings and to catch up on the latest gossip. There were also rooms where you could sit quietly, exercise areas and gardens to walk about in. Only the very rich had their own baths because everyone enjoyed their visit to the public baths.*

The House of Diana at Ostia. The ground floor was used as a row of shops, while above them were apartments. Buildings at Ostia rarely rose above four storeys and were built of plastered red or yellow bricks. Roman *insulae* could be over six storeys in height.

City Life

At its peak, Rome was so crowded that most people lived in *insulae*, high rise blocks of five or six storeys. Between the blocks were narrow alleyways which let in hardly any sunlight. The upper floors had no running water or sanitation, so people collected their water from public fountains, used public toilets and threw their waste out of their windows or into a well inside the building. To us, Rome would have seemed a noisy, smelly place. During the day it was so busy that vehicles were banned, and goods were only allowed to be brought into the city at night.

The heart of the city was the Forum, a grand open space where public meetings were held. Around the Forum were the Basilicas where law courts were held. Scattered throughout the city were the huge public buildings erected by the various emperors, and the temples to the gods. Beside these were the *insulae*. Their lower storeys were shops or businesses or even the grand apartments of rich people.

The Villa Julia Felix and its garden were built in Pompeii. Pompeii was a small provincial city whose chief product was cloth. Houses here were built in a quadrangle style enclosing a small garden.

Poorer people lived above the first floor and had no cooking facilities. The *insulae* often collapsed or burnt down. Alongside them, the houses of the rich were low buildings with windowless outer walls. Inside was an open courtyard with a pool, the *impluvium*, to catch rainwater. Around the courtyard were the dining room, kitchen, toilet and various sitting rooms. The house was entered by a gate in the wall. The family shrine was in the garden behind the house. In some of the colder countries of the Empire the house was heated by a hypocaust system. Air, warmed by a furnace, travelled around underfloor passages and up through ducts in the walls.

Fires were a daily occurrence in Rome. The poet Juvenal wrote: 'No, no, I must live where there is no fire and the night is free from alarms'. The upper storeys of buildings were mostly made of wood and had no water supply. They were heated, if at all, by open braziers of coal and lit by oil lamps. Fire-fighting consisted of teams of slaves or soldiers forming chains with buckets of water.

Country Life

Many wealthy Roman citizens had houses in the countryside. After the wars with Carthage it became fashionable for retiring generals, with lots of loot from the wars, to build great country estates. Their villas were enclosed by walls; at one end of the enclosure was the villa where the owner lived, at the other end would be the buildings where the slaves and animals lived. There was a storehouse, rooms for fermenting wine and pressing olive oil, and a bath house which would be used by both the owner and the servants. Around the villa, olives, grapes, figs, vegetables and grain were grown. Bees were kept for their honey, and there would usually be large herds of pigs, because pork was the favourite meat of the Romans. Sheep and goats were kept to produce wool, rope and milk, while cattle and donkeys were beasts of burden.

▶ This mosaic, from Tunis in North Africa, shows the activities of a working villa. The villa in the centre is surrounded by scenes of agricultural life: slaves gathering food, administration tasks, hunting and looking after livestock.

▼ People who lived in the city, like the Emperor Hadrian, often had villas in the countryside. Hadrian's villa was so grand that it was more of a palace than a country home.

Pigeons, ducks, geese and hens were kept on the estates for food and feathers.

Whether on a grand estate or a tiny farm, many of the tools that Roman farmers used were very similar to the ones still used today. To till the soil they used a plough pulled by oxen. To break up stony land they had picks. The crops were harvested using a sickle, but some of the big farms had threshing machines. Flour mill wheels were turned by an animal such as a donkey. Wine was a favourite product of Italy, and grapes were grown in many farms; when they were ripe they were put into a stone trough and trodden to extract the juice. The Romans were quite sophisticated farmers; they practised crop rotation to improve the soil.

Hadrian's Villa at Tivoli, north east of Rome, is a fine example of a Roman villa at its grandest. As well as all the usual rooms the villa had a library, a theatre and a stadium, while the ornamental gardens around his house covered an area of 18 km^2.

In a book on farm management written by Marcus Cato, the duties of a farm manager, who was usually a slave, are described:

'The farm manager must not be an idler… He must be the first to rise in the morning and the last to bed. He must see that the farm is shut up and that everyone is asleep in the right place and the animals have fodder.'

In his book on farm management Cato advises on the best treatment of slaves: 'Each slave in the chain gang should have 1.5 kg of bread each day during winter, and 2 kg when they begin work in the vineyard.' He also recommends that slaves should get a new set of clothes every two years. The slaves who worked on these farms had a hard life, often kept in chain gangs and locked up at night to prevent them from escaping.

▲ This is part of a floor mosaic, perhaps from a dining room. It shows seafood delicacies such as lobster, octopus and eels. These might have been part of the main course of the meal, served in rich sauces. Some people enjoyed their meal so much that they took medicine half way through to make themselves vomit. That way they could go back and start all over again!

Food

The type of food eaten by the citizens of Rome was determined by how rich they were. Very poor people were given free handouts of grain or bread, sometimes even wine and oil. City working people bought cooked food from stalls in the street: circular loaves of bread, hot cooked turnips, eggs, sausages or pease pudding. Meat was rarely eaten. Rich people had teams of slaves to prepare elaborate, sumptuous meals. Their food was cooked in spices and herbs such as coriander, nutmeg, cumin, ginger, mint and thyme, and served with fish or fruit sauces. Some slaves spent their whole day preparing the evening meal for their masters.

The evening meal consisted of three courses. Starters were items like salad or snails or shellfish. Wine sweetened with honey was served after this. The next course was several dishes of different meats served with vegetables and sauces. The last course might be fruit, honey and cakes, or stuffed dates. Wine was served throughout the meal. During a dinner party there would usually be a poetry reading or musical performance of some kind.

Clothes

Roman men wore quite simple clothes. Their underwear was just a loincloth, and over that they wore a short, woollen tunic. When they went out they wore a toga – a large sheet of cloth draped in elaborate folds around the shoulders. Most people hated to wear it and various emperors had to pass laws forcing men to put on their togas for public occasions. In Britain and other cold areas of the Empire, men needed to wear tight-fitting leggings, warm socks, and even a waterproof cape.

In the early days of the Empire Roman women kept their hair in a simple knot, but later elaborate braids and curls and blonde or red wigs were popular. Women used ash or antimony (a type of metal) to darken their eyelids; and the sediment from red wine or red ochre for lipstick. They often covered their faces in powdered chalk to whiten them and carried little sets of tools for plucking hair and cleaning out ears. Jewellery was important. Women often wore earrings made of gold, set with precious stones, and gold link chains round their necks. Brooches might be cameos carved from sardonyx or precious gems. Women also wore anklets and bracelets; a snake design was very popular for these. It was the custom to wear a wedding ring and probably several other rings, often between the first and second joints of the fingers.

▲ Heated metal curling tongs were used to create complicated hairstyles like this one. Red or blonde hair for making wigs was often taken from the heads of foreign slaves.

Women wore a loincloth and brassiere. Over this they too wore a tunic. Married women wore another gown called a *stola* which was a long overdress. When they went out they wore a *palla* which was a shawl which they draped in various styles around their shoulders and heads.

Entertainment

The most popular forms of entertainment in ancient Rome were chariot racing and the games. They took place on the 150 or more annual public holidays that Rome had. They were paid for by rich men or by the government, who wanted to keep the poor people of Rome contented. These big spectacles were immensely popular. In 160 BC, during a performance of a play by Terence, someone announced that the chariot races were starting, and the entire audience ran out of the theatre! The chariot races took place at the Circus Maximus, with slaves as drivers. If they were successful these men grew very rich and famous; but the chariots often crashed and the drivers were killed or injured. Fans of one chariot team would often get into fights with fans of another.

▼ In the chariot races teams of four horses pulled a tiny chariot driven by a slave. The course has three pillars at each end and in the middle a man is counting the laps. Three of the seven laps have been run in this picture as there are four markers still left. At the three pillars the chariots had to make a 180° turn which was very dangerous – many men died doing this.

The games that were held in the Colosseum were even more horrific. Criminals or slaves were given weapons and put into the ring to fight to the death. They were called gladiators. Those who refused to fight were pushed into the ring with red hot irons.

► Here we can see armed gladiators fighting wild animals. Often the humans would be bound to stakes and left to be torn apart, but here they are able to defend themselves.

Although many gladiators became rich and famous and received their freedom, life would have been desperate for most of them. In 73 BC a group of gladiators in Capua broke out of their prison and escaped. They were led by a man from Thrace, called Spartacus. He had fought for the Roman army and had considerable skills as a general. He knew that if he was caught he would be killed. Thousands of slaves all over Italy deserted from their farms and joined him. Roman armies were sent out to capture them and were beaten. The band of runaways rampaged around the countryside, travelling north towards the Alps and robbing farms on their way. Spartacus tried to persuade them to flee over the Alps to freedom, but many of them were enjoying their life as bandits too much. They were eventually defeated, and while most, including Spartacus, fought to the death, 6,000 were captured and crucified along the main road into Rome, as a warning to other slaves.

At the games an unarmed man was usually pitted against one in armour. Often men were put into the arena so the audience could watch them being mauled to death by wild animals. In AD 80, 5,000 wild animals and 4,000 tame animals were killed in just one day.

A very popular form of the games was when the Colosseum was flooded, or a nearby lake was used, and teams of slaves in boats fought one another. People enjoyed betting on the races and games. Spectators occasionally got injured. Once, in AD 27, an entire amphitheatre collapsed, killing 50,000 people. Another time a herd of elephants stampeded, breaking down the barriers which protected the crowds and injuring many people.

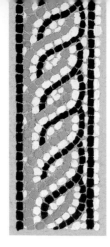

CHAPTER 9

Decline and Fall

Decline of the Empire

As the Empire grew and grew, many things changed in Rome – not always for the better. Ambitious soldiers and provincial governors fought to be the next emperor. As we have seen, many of the emperors were bad, while some were good administrators who strengthened the Empire. After the death of Marcus Aurelius, Rome was plagued by a series of poor rulers. The first of these was Marcus Aurelius' son, who ruled Rome for 12 years and was one of the worst emperors that the Empire had ever seen. He was eventually assassinated by the Praetorian Guard, who auctioned off the job of Emperor to the highest bidder! During the following century so much time was spent fighting over who would be emperor, that little care was paid to the far reaches of the Empire.

In Germany, local tribes called the Goths, the Franks and the Alamanni banded together and began to threaten Roman territory.

Marcus Aurelius, a Spaniard from Cordoba, served as emperor from AD 161 to 180. He was a very shy man who, before becoming emperor, had spent his life studying philosophy. He inherited an empire which had little money to spend and several wars to fight. One of his ways of finding cash was to sell off the imperial jewels. He oversaw a war against the Parthians in AD 163-4, and although his troops were successful, they brought a terrible plague back to Rome, which spread across the empire and killed thousands of people. On the German front, Marcus Aurelius sent troops against the Marcomanni and Quadi tribes and defeated them. He built a column in Rome to celebrate his victory. During his time as emperor he wrote a book of philosophy, in Greek.

In Parthia there were constant battles and in AD 259 the Emperor Valerian was actually captured by the Persians. In AD 270 the Emperor Aurelian abandoned Dacia and concentrated his efforts on defeating the Alamanni on the German border. He also reconquered Gaul which had declared itself independent of Rome. Then Queen Zenobia of Palmyra, to the east of the Empire, began attacks on Egypt and Asia Minor. She too was defeated by Aurelian, and her city destroyed. Aurelian remained emperor for 14 years, but he too was assassinated.

▼ Zenobia was Queen of Palmyra, the oasis city in northern Arabia, which was a vital stopping point on the Roman caravan routes. It was destroyed after its attacks on the empire.

◀ Marcus Aurelius' column in Rome was erected in AD 176. It celebrates his triumph over the Marcomanni. Near the top we can see soldiers holding their shields in a tortoise formation. Their shields are locked together in a defensive posture.

▼ The early Christian symbols of chi (X) and rho (P), adopted by Constantine, can be seen here. Alongside them are the letters alpha (A) and omega (Ω), the first and last letters of the Greek alphabet, symbolizing the beginning and end of life.

A Divided Empire

After the assassination of Aurelian, in AD 275, there was another scramble for power and Rome became very unstable once again. Food prices began to rise and heavy taxes were introduced. Bands of outlaws began to roam around the Empire, and fresh invasions began around the borders. In AD 284 Diocletian came to power. His solution to the problem of keeping the Empire together was to split it into two sections – the east and the west – and to have two emperors. He strengthened the army, set maximum prices for food and set a limit for wage rises. His solutions did little to solve any of Rome's problems, but they did make the army more powerful and dangerous. The senate lost a lot of its power during this period. Black markets for food and other goods began. Diocletian declared himself a god, and in AD 305 retired to a great palace in the modern town of Split in Croatia. Chaos broke out again with up to four contenders for the job of emperor at any one time, until in AD 312 the general in charge of Britain, Constantine, returned to Rome to claim the throne. After winning a battle with his chief rival for power in Rome, Maxentius, he declared tolerance for all religious groups. He slowly reunited the various bits of the Empire, brought in higher taxes, made the army more powerful and took away lots of the freedoms that Romans were used to. But his measures did not restore the strength of the Empire.

Christians had been persecuted in the Roman Empire since the very early days. Despite this, the religion had grown. When Constantine left Britain and was about to begin the battle for Rome, he thought he saw a vision in the sky. He believed he saw a cross, and the words, in hoc signo vinces *meaning, 'you will conquer with this sign'. After his success in battle he allowed Christians to worship one god. Later he even made himself the head of the Christian church in Rome. This meant that the state god – the emperor – was also the leader of the Christians and so it made Christianity much more important in the Roman Empire. He adopted the Christian symbol of the first two letters of Christ's name. They are X and P in Greek. They can be seen in many decorations of the time.*

▼ This is what remains of a once huge statue of Constantine which was probably worshipped as the image of a god.

The western part of the Empire was constantly under attack from the Barbarians (the name the Romans gave to the various tribes around their borders). Constantine realized that he could not prevent it from being taken, so he moved his capital city away from Rome to Byzantium in the east, and renamed it Constantinople. In that way he kept the Roman Empire alive for another thousand years.

▼ The Emperor Justinian was the son of a Slav peasant. Also shown in the mosaic is his general Belisarius. The name Maximian appears above the Archbishop.

The Sack of Rome

Constantine chose his three sons to become emperors after him, but the Empire quickly fell victim to more power struggles. The worst threat to the Empire, especially the western half of it, was invasion. A tribe of nomads from the east, called the Huns, were moving across Europe looking for fresh land; as they marched on they chased the German tribes in front of them. Tribes such as the Vandals, Visigoths and Suebi fled to the Empire for protection from the Huns, and were allowed to settle there. They joined the Roman armies. Later, even Huns who had crossed into Roman territory were allowed to stay and defend the borders. Weak emperors had no finances to drive out the enemies of Rome, so they were forced to accept them.

In AD 402, Italy was invaded by the Goths. Rome was still the capital of the western Empire, but the emperor, Honorius, was afraid and moved to Ravenna on the east coast of Italy. In AD 409 Vandals invaded Spain. The following year Rome was sacked and looted by the Goths and the Roman legions were withdrawn from Britain to defend Italy.

Constantine's foresight in moving the capital of the empire to safety, in Byzantium, meant that while Roman buildings and laws fell apart in the west, the east was flourishing. Latin died out as the dominant language and was replaced by Greek; and art and architecture gradually grew away from its Roman origins. The last great emperor of Constantinople was Justinian, from AD 527–565, who sent troops back to Europe to reclaim the western empire. The cost of the operation was much too high, and too much damage had been done in Rome and the great cities of North Africa. Within 100 years the cities were all lost again. Justinian also reformed and rewrote all the Roman laws, and his legal code is the basis of modern European law today.

Northern Europe was then taken over by the Franks, North Africa by the Vandals and France by Attila the Hun. Finally Ravenna, the new capital, was taken, and the emperor deposed in AD 476. This signalled the absolute end of the original western Roman Empire.

▼ By AD 500 the Roman Empire existed only in the east, and western Europe was divided into smaller kingdoms ruled by the invaders from the north.

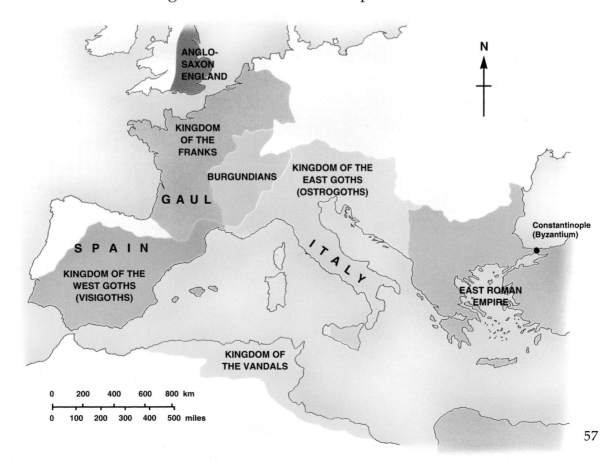

57

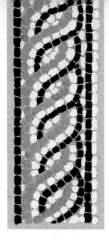

CHAPTER 10

The Roman Legacy

Roman Influence

Roman civilization lasted for over 1,000 years and affected the lives of millions of people. It brought cities to rural Europe and brought people who were hundreds of miles apart, with different languages and beliefs, into one big community. Strangely, when the Romans withdrew from a city their technology left with them, and people fell back into barbarism. Their beautiful buildings could not be maintained, their plumbing fell into disrepair and their aqueducts stopped working.

Even today the Romans influence our daily lives. The language that we speak has many of its roots in Latin. The Roman name for an apartment block, *insula*, meaning a building separated from those around it, has given us the word 'insulate'. The Roman common man, *plebeian*, has come directly into our language and has also given us the word 'plebiscite', meaning a vote taken by all the people. The Roman word for father, *pater*, has given us many words like 'paternal', 'patriotic', 'patronize' and 'patron'. It would be very difficult to speak even one sentence without using a word which has its roots in Latin. Other modern languages like Spanish, French and Italian are even closer to Latin.

Although the Roman Empire ended a long time ago, we know a great deal about it. When the Romans adopted Christianity they set up many monasteries where monks spent a lot of their time copying out famous books. Alongside Christian books, much of ancient Roman literature was also preserved, and that is how we know the history of ancient Rome.

▲ Roads built by the Romans, like this one in Yorkshire in England, have survived to the present day.

The Romans have left us many other things besides their language. The European legal system is based on the Roman one. Our ideas about government and legal institutions have also come from the Romans. Their contribution to transport was great too; Roman roads are still the basis of many European highways. One of the first roads built in Britain was Watling Street, which runs from the south coast in Kent to Chester in the Midlands. Nowadays it is called the A5. Some Roman buildings are actually still in use, such as Diocletian's Palace in Split. The jury system, the postal service, the fire service, daily newspapers, central heating, flushing toilets and apartment blocks can all be traced back to the Romans too.

▲ Communal public flushing toilets, such as this one, became common in Rome – even in private houses, where they could seat up to 20 people at a time. A channel of running water flows underneath the toilet and a smaller channel can be seen in front of the toilet for washing after use.

We have also learned much about the Romans by looking at the ruins of their cities and towns. In marble statues we can see records of important events, or we can read the inscriptions on Roman graves. From the pictures on unearthed mosaic floors we can learn things about everyday life. An incredible piece of the past has been preserved in the remains of Pompeii. One afternoon in AD 79, without warning, this town was covered in ash by the eruption of Mount Vesuvius and left intact. The ash preserved the town exactly as it had been, with everyone going about their business. The town remains today, with food still on the tables, graffiti still on the walls and houses laid out as they were on the day of the eruption. Even people and dogs, running away from the horror of the volcano, were covered in ash and lie exactly where they died centuries ago. Today tourists walk among the ruins of the town and imagine the Romans going about their daily routines.

▼ This is one of the 2,000 or more residents of Pompeii who didn't make it to the boats in time. He was probably suffocated by the dust which fell on to the city, eventually covering it.

Timeline

149–146 Last war against Carthage. The city is destroyed.
133 Plans to reallocate land in Rome to the poor are abandoned.
73 Slave revolt led by Spartacus.
67 Pompey is given the task of getting rid of pirates in the Mediterranean.

27 Augustus becomes 'first citizen'.
4 The birth of Christ.

BC
753 According to legend, Rome is founded by Romulus and Remus.
510 The Roman Republic established.
451 The Twelve Tablets are written down.
386 Rome is attacked by the Gauls.
367 The first *plebeian* is elected consul.
343–290 Wars against the Samnites.
282–275 Wars against the Greeks.
264–241 First war against Carthage.
238 Corsica and Sardinia made into Roman provinces.
218–202 Hannibal's armies in Italy.
201 End of the second war against Carthage.

58 Gaius Julius Caesar is made governor of Gaul.
45 Julius Caesar takes power in Rome.
44 Julius Caesar is murdered.

AD
29 Christ is crucified.
43 Claudius invades Britain.
64 Great Fire of Rome.
122 Hadrian's Wall is started.
376 Goths invade Italy and sack Rome.
395 The Empire is divided.
476 The last Roman emperor is deposed.

Glossary

Amphitheatre A round, roofless theatre with steep banks of seats built around a circular arena. It was used for the Games.

Amphora A pottery jar used for keeping liquids such as olive oil and wine in.

Circus Maximus A huge chariot racing arena in Rome.

Consul The top government job in Rome, usually held by two men elected for one year.

Corbita A Roman trading ship.

Equites A class of Roman citizens made up of the wealthy middle class businessmen.

Etruscans People who settled in north west and central Italy in 800 BC. They were the early kings of Rome.

Fasces A bundle of rods with an axe in the middle symbolising the authority of a high magistrate.

Hastati Roman soldiers who wore light armour and carried a sword and javelin.

Honestiores A class of person who would receive a light sentence for his crimes.

Humiliores A class of person who would be punished more heavily for his crimes.

Hypocaust Roman central heating using an underground furnace to send hot air under the floors of a building.

Insula A Roman block of flats.

Isis An Egyptian goddess worshipped by the Romans.

Lares Roman gods of the household.

Lictor A servant who carried the magistrate's fasces.

Mosaic A floor covering made from tiny pieces of tile or stone.

Nobiles The highest class of Roman citizen.

Papyrus Writing paper made from the leaves of a water plant from Egypt.

Paterfamilias The head of a Roman family.

Patricians The Roman upper class who in early times held power in Rome.

Penates Roman gods who protected a family's larder.

Plebeian A common working man.

Principes Roman soldiers armed with sword , spear and shield.

Quadrangle A rectangular courtyard with buildings on all four sides.

Senate A council of 300 or more important citizens which advised the consuls or the Emperor.

Strigil A curved scraper for cleaning the skin.

Theatre A semicircular roofless building with steep banks of seats and a stage across the straight side. Plays were staged in the theatre.

Toga A Roman man's outer garment.

Triarii Roman soldiers armed with spear and protected by armour.

Tribune Representative of the *Plebeians*, first elected in 490 BC.

Triclinium A dining room with three sofas around a table.

Velites The poorest kind of Roman soldier with no armour, just a spear.

Further Reading

A Roman Town by Jonathan Rutland (Hutchinson & Co, 1977)

Ancient Rome (Eyewitness Guides) by Simon James (Dorling Kindersley, 1990)

Growing Up in Ancient Rome by Mike Corbishley (Eagle Books, 1993)

Hannibal & the Enemies of Rome by Peter Connolly (Macdonald Educational, 1978)

The Romans by John Haywood (Simon & Schuster, 1994)

The Romans by Anthony Marks & Graham Tingay (Usborne Publishing, 1990)

The Romans (Usborne Hotshots) by Philippa Wingate (Usborne Publishing, 1995)

The Roman Army by Peter Connolly (Simon & Schuster, 1989)

The Roman Empire & the Dark Ages by Giovanni Caselli (Macdonald, 1981)

The Rotten Romans by Terry Deary (Scholastic, 1993)

Tiberius Claudius Maximus The Legionary by Peter Connolly (Oxford University Press, 1988)

What Do We Know About The Romans? by Mike Corbishley (Simon & Schuster, 1991)

Index

Figures in bold are illustrations